HOUSE-HUNTING NOTEBOOK

www.wildrose-media.com

House-Hunting Notebook: Property Comparison Checklists and More

ISBN: 978-1-953489-30-2

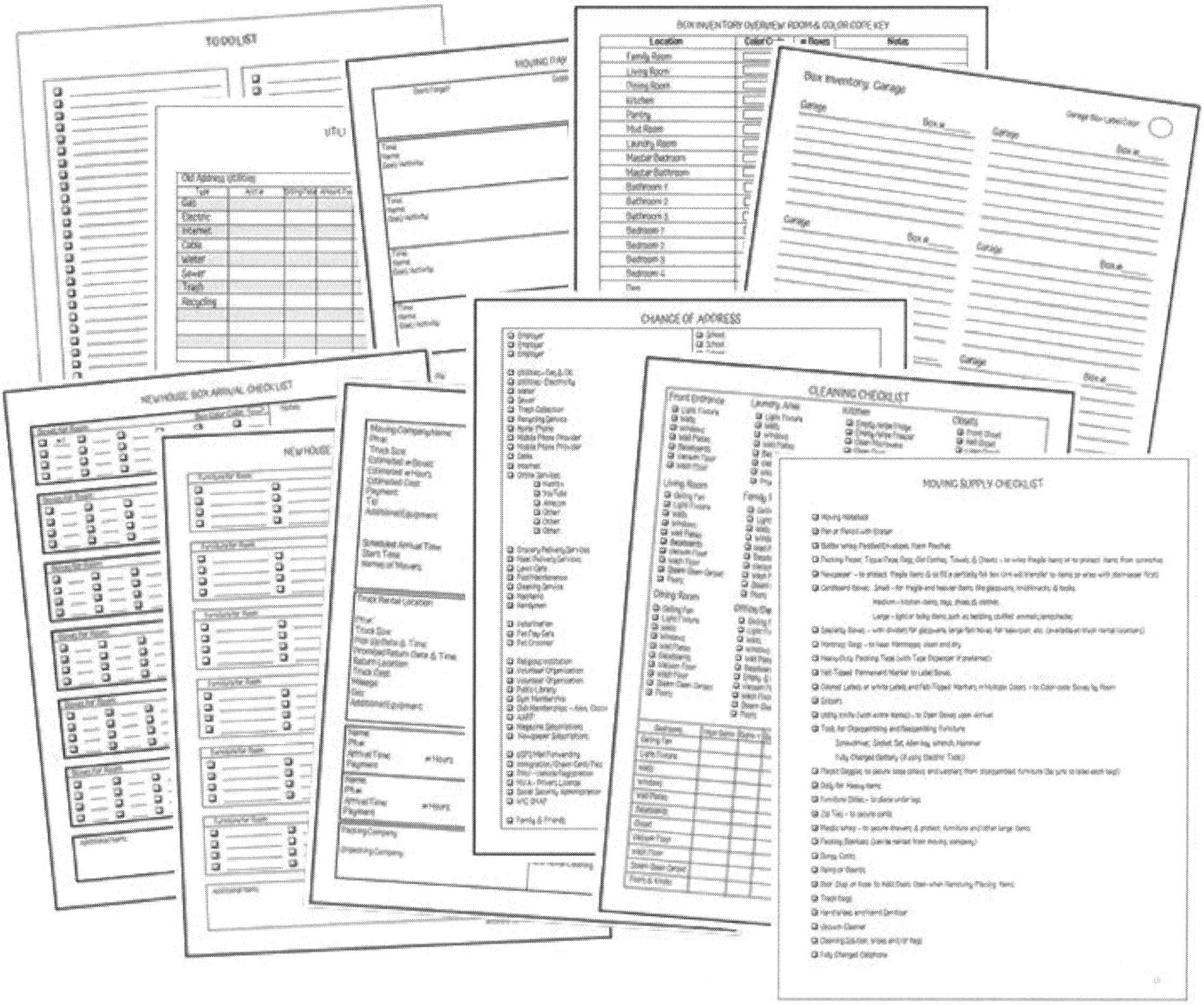
TO DO LIST
BOX INVENTORY OVERVIEW ROOM & COLOR CODE KEY
Box Inventory: Garage
CHANGE OF ADDRESS
CLEANING CHECKLIST
MOVING SUPPLY CHECKLIST

REALTOR CONTACT INFORMATION

Company Name:
Agent's Name:
Realtor Ph #:
Date Contacted:
Home Search Began:

Automated Online Search - Email Used:
Search Parameters:

Online Search Results:

Company Name:
Agent's Name:
Realtor Ph #:
Date Contacted:
Home Search Began:

Automated Online Search - Email Used:
Search Parameters:

Online Search Results:

Company Name:
Agent's Name:
Realtor Ph #:
Date Contacted:
Home Search Began:

Automated Online Search - Email Used:
Search Parameters:

Online Search Results:

NEW HOME WISH LIST IDEAS

GENERAL

Single Family Home
Duplex
Multi-Family
Townhouse/Row Home
Condominium
Apartment
High-Rise
Acreage/Farm Land - # acres ______
Off-Grid

Budget - Mortgage Payment
HOA or. No HOA

Move-in Ready
Needs Paint and Décor
Fixer-Upper
Complete Renovation
Tear-Down and Build New

One-Story / Two Story / Penthouse
End of Row Unit / Middle Unit
Handicap Accessible - Ramp
Handicap Accessible - Elevator
Secure Building
Concierge Service / Doorman
Fitness Facility
Meeting Room
On-Site Daycare

External Door Dead Bolts
Security System
Intercom
Heat Source - Electric - Gas
- Propane - Solar
Fire Place: Wood - Electric - Gas
Wood-Burning or Pellet Stove

Handicap Accessible/Ramp
Elevator
Walk-Up
Central Air Conditioning
Ceiling Fans
200 AMP Electric
400 AMP Electric
GFI Outlets
Sump Pump

Appliances Included
Whole House Water Filtration

Home Warranty

INTERIOR

Home Size - Min/Max Square Feet
Bedrooms
Bathrooms

Décor - Neutral Colors
- Modern
- Vintage

Open Floor Plan
Flooring Material
French / Barn / Pocket Doors

Sitting Area in Master Bedroom
Two Master Suites
Main Floor Bedroom(s)

Closets - Walk-In
- Hall / Linen Closet
- Front Entrance

Kitchen Eat-In Kitchen
Kitchen Island
Stove - Gas - Electric
Double Ovens
Double / Deep Sink
Instant Hot Water
Water Filtration
Window Over Sink
Cabinet Space
Counter Space
Countertop Material
Pantry

Bathroom Double Sinks
Separate Shower & Tub
Separate Toilet Area
Jetted /Claw Foot Tub
Large Shower
Shower Doors/Curtain
Bathroom Storage/Linen Closet

Laundry Room Location
Washer/Dryer
Laundry Shoot
Utility Sink
Folding Space
Storage
Mud Room
Office Space
Theater/Movie Room
Playroom
Craft Room
School / Classroom

Good Light for House Plants
Windows - Type, Size, & Location
Sky Lights
High-Speed Internet Connection

Basement - Finished
- Unfinished
Basement Access - Interior
- Exterior
Basement: In-Law Suite

Root Cellar
Storm Shelter
Attic Space & Access
Screened-in Porch
Sun Room/Florida Room

EXTERIOR

Low-Maintenance Exterior
Siding - Clap Board - Cedar
Brick - Stone - Stucco - Log

Front / Side/ Back Porch
Patio or Deck for BBQ
Balcony

Yard Size & Maintenance
Hardscape
Grass
Low-Water Landscaping
Vegetable Garden
Flower Garden
Fruit Trees
Berry Bushes

Sprinkler System
Irrigation System

Fence / Gate
Greenhouse
Workshop
Storage Shed
Dog/Cat Run
Chicken Coop
Play House / Tree House
Swing Set
Sand Box

Well
Septic System
Energy Saving Features
Solar Panels
Generator

Pool
Hot Tub
Sauna/Steam Room
Hose Access to wash vehicles
On Snow Route
Fire pit (or room to build one)
Pier - Do ck - Boat Lift
Pond

PARKING

On or Off-Street Parking
Parking Spaces
Circular Drive
Covered Parking
Garage: 1-Car 2-Car 3-Car
Garage with Electricity
Block Heater Outlet for Vehicle
Electric Vehicle Charging Station
RV Parking
Boat Parking

LOCATION

Privacy - Proximity to Neighbors
Quiet - Proximity to Fire Station
Safe Neighborhood
In City - Suburbs - Rural
Specific Location/Development

Located in a Cul de Sac
On a Dead End Road
No Speed Bumps on Street
No Bus Stop Near Home (noise)
Has Multiple Road Access

Walkable
Bikeable
Near Family
Near School
Near Work
Near Childcare Provider
Near Church/Worship Center
Near Hospital/Physician/Vet
Near Public Transport
Near Library
Near Gym/Rec Center
Near Shopping Center
Near Grocery Store
Near Sports Center
Near Shipping Center/USPS
Near Boat Ramp/Fishing Pier
Near Beach/Lake
Near Airport/Train Station

ADDITIONAL WANTS & NEEDS

NEW HOME WISH LIST

LOCATION

MUST HAVE	WOULD LIKE TO HAVE

EXTERIOR

MUST HAVE	WOULD LIKE TO HAVE

INTERIOR

MUST HAVE	WOULD LIKE TO HAVE

NEW HOME WISH LIST

LOCATION

MUST HAVE	WOULD LIKE TO HAVE

EXTERIOR

MUST HAVE	WOULD LIKE TO HAVE

INTERIOR

MUST HAVE	WOULD LIKE TO HAVE

DECISION-MAKING WORKSHEET

Pros	Cons

Notes

HOUSE EVALUATION FORM

Address: ______________________ MLS#: __________
Neighborhood: ______________ HOA Fees: ________ Annual Taxes: ________
Asking Price: ________ Days on the Market: ______ Square Feet: ________ Price Per Square Foot: ________
Bedrooms: ________ Lot Size: __________ Year Built: ______
Bathrooms: ________ Price Changes: ______________

LOAN: Conv · FHA · VA · USDA · Cash · 203K
FS By Owner · REO · Foreclosure · Auction

Home Type: single family · duplex · condo · townhome · mobile
Foundation: slab · block · brick · stone · poured concrete
Basement Space: none · crawl space · partial · full · cellar
Basement: interior access · exterior access · finished · unfinished
Air Conditioning: none · central · window · mini split · fans

Garage: yes · no attached · detached #Parking Spaces: ______
Wheelchair Access: yes · no · ramp · elevator #Steps to Door: ______
Water: municipal · well · none Well: pump age: _____ #gal/min: ____
Waste: municipal · septic drain field/holding tank #gallons: ________
Heat: electric · gas · oil · propane · fireplace/stove · pellet stove · solar

Appointment Date/Time: ______________ Realtor's Name: ______________
Meet Location: ______________ Realtor's Number: ______________

Notes

OVERALL IMPRESSION

☆ ☆ ☆ ☆ ☆

MAKE OFFER • MAYBE • DISCARD

INDOOR EVALUATION

ROOM/LOCATION	CONDITION			NOTES
	good	fair	poor	flooring - paint - lighting
Front Entrance				
Living Room				
Dining Room				
Kitchen				
Pantry				
Family Room				
Master Bedroom				
Master Bathroom				
2nd Bedroom				
3rd Bedroom				
4th Bedroom				
Bathroom 1				
Bathroom 2				
Bathroom 3				
Laundry Area				
Mud Room				
Office/Den				
Library				
Utilities				
Basement				

EXTERIOR and YARD EVALUATION

LOCATION	NOTES
Curb Appeal	
Roof	
Windows	
Front Entrance	
Landscaping	
Trees/Shrubs	
Yard	
Lighting	
Garage	
Shed	
Deck/Patio	

OTHER CONSIDERATIONS

Neighborhood:
Cul de Sac · Dead End Road · Through Street · Rural
Safety Score: ________ Walkability Score: ________
Proximity to: Work · School · Family · Babysitter
Bus Stop · Public Transportation · Grocery Store
Schools: Elementary ______________
Middle ______________
High ______________
School District: Walk · Bus
Noise: Traffic · Business · Sirens-Police/Firehouse · Kids · Dogs
Privacy: Proximity to Neighbor · Fence · Fence Height

DECISION-MAKING WORKSHEET

Pros	Cons

Notes

HOUSE EVALUATION FORM

Address: ______________________ MLS#: __________
Neighborhood: ______________________ HOA Fees: __________ Annual Taxes: __________
Asking Price: __________ Days on the Market: __________ Square Feet: __________ Price Per Square Foot: __________
Bedrooms: __________ Lot Size: __________ Year Built: __________
Bathrooms: __________ Price Changes: ______________________

LOAN: Conv · FHA · VA · USDA · Cash · 203K
FS By Owner · REO · Foreclosure · Auction

Home Type: single family · duplex · condo · townhome · mobile
Foundation: slab · block · brick · stone · poured concrete
Basement Space: none · crawl space · partial · full · cellar
Basement: interior access · exterior access · finished · unfinished
Air Conditioning: none · central · window · mini split · fans

Garage: yes · no attached · detached #Parking Spaces: ______
Wheelchair Access: yes · no · ramp · elevator #Steps to Door: ______
Water: municipal · well · none Well: pump age: _____ #gal/min: ____
Waste: municipal · septic drain field/holding tank #gallons: ________
Heat: electric · gas · oil · propane · fireplace/stove · pellet stove · solar

Appointment Date/Time: ______________________ Realtor's Name: ______________________
Meet Location: ______________________ Realtor's Number: ______________________

Notes

OVERALL IMPRESSION

☆☆☆☆☆

MAKE OFFER • MAYBE • DISCARD

INDOOR EVALUATION

ROOM/LOCATION	CONDITION			NOTES
	good	fair	poor	flooring - paint - lighting
Front Entrance				
Living Room				
Dining Room				
Kitchen				
Pantry				
Family Room				
Master Bedroom				
Master Bathroom				
2nd Bedroom				
3rd Bedroom				
4th Bedroom				
Bathroom 1				
Bathroom 2				
Bathroom 3				
Laundry Area				
Mud Room				
Office/Den				
Library				
Utilities				
Basement				

EXTERIOR and YARD EVALUATION

LOCATION	NOTES
Curb Appeal	
Roof	
Windows	
Front Entrance	
Landscaping	
Trees/Shrubs	
Yard	
Lighting	
Garage	
Shed	
Deck/Patio	

OTHER CONSIDERATIONS

Neighborhood:
Cul de Sac · Dead End Road · Through Street · Rural
Safety Score: ________ Walkability Score: ________
Proximity to: Work · School · Family · Babysitter
Bus Stop · Public Transportation · Grocery Store
Schools: Elementary ______________________
Middle ______________________
High ______________________
School District: Walk · Bus
Noise: Traffic · Business · Sirens-Police/Firehouse · Kids · Dogs
Privacy: Proximity to Neighbor · Fence · Fence Height

DECISION-MAKING WORKSHEET

Pros	Cons

Notes

HOUSE EVALUATION FORM

Address: ______________________ MLS#: ____________
Neighborhood: ______________ HOA Fees: __________ Annual Taxes: __________
Asking Price: __________ Days on the Market: ______ Square Feet: ________ Price Per Square Foot: ________
Bedrooms: __________ Lot Size: __________ Year Built: ______
Bathrooms: __________ Price Changes: ______________

LOAN: Conv · FHA · VA · USDA · Cash · 203K
FS By Owner · REO · Foreclosure · Auction

Home Type: single family · duplex · condo · townhome · mobile
Foundation: slab · block · brick · stone · poured concrete
Basement Space: none · crawl space · partial · full · cellar
Basement: interior access · exterior access · finished · unfinished
Air Conditioning: none · central · window · mini split · fans

Garage: yes · no attached · detached #Parking Spaces: ______
Wheelchair Access: yes · no · ramp · elevator #Steps to Door: ______
Water: municipal · well · none Well: pump age: _____ #gal/min: ____
Waste: municipal · septic drain field/holding tank #gallons: ________
Heat: electric · gas · oil · propane · fireplace/stove · pellet stove · solar

Appointment Date/Time: ______________ Realtor's Name: ______________
Meet Location: ______________ Realtor's Number: ______________

Notes

OVERALL IMPRESSION

☆ ☆ ☆ ☆ ☆

MAKE OFFER • MAYBE • DISCARD

INDOOR EVALUATION

ROOM/LOCATION	CONDITION			NOTES
	good	fair	poor	flooring - paint - lighting
Front Entrance				
Living Room				
Dining Room				
Kitchen				
Pantry				
Family Room				
Master Bedroom				
Master Bathroom				
2nd Bedroom				
3rd Bedroom				
4th Bedroom				
Bathroom 1				
Bathroom 2				
Bathroom 3				
Laundry Area				
Mud Room				
Office/Den				
Library				
Utilities				
Basement				

EXTERIOR and YARD EVALUATION

LOCATION	NOTES
Curb Appeal	
Roof	
Windows	
Front Entrance	
Landscaping	
Trees/Shrubs	
Yard	
Lighting	
Garage	
Shed	
Deck/Patio	

OTHER CONSIDERATIONS

Neighborhood:
Cul de Sac · Dead End Road · Through Street · Rural
Safety Score: ________ Walkability Score: ________
Proximity to: Work · School · Family · Babysitter
Bus Stop · Public Transportation · Grocery Store
Schools: Elementary ______________
Middle ______________
High ______________
School District: Walk · Bus
Noise: Traffic · Business · Sirens-Police/Firehouse · Kids · Dogs
Privacy: Proximity to Neighbor · Fence · Fence Height

DECISION-MAKING WORKSHEET

Pros	Cons

Notes

HOUSE EVALUATION FORM

Address: ______________________________ MLS#: __________
Neighborhood: __________________ HOA Fees: __________ Annual Taxes: __________
Asking Price: __________ Days on the Market: ______ Square Feet: __________ Price Per Square Foot: __________
Bedrooms: __________ Lot Size: __________ Year Built: ______
Bathrooms: __________ Price Changes: __________________

LOAN: Conv · FHA · VA · USDA · Cash · 203K
FS By Owner · REO · Foreclosure · Auction

Home Type: single family · duplex · condo · townhome · mobile
Foundation: slab · block · brick · stone · poured concrete
Basement Space: none · crawl space · partial · full · cellar
Basement: interior access · exterior access · finished · unfinished
Air Conditioning: none · central · window · mini split · fans

Garage: yes · no attached · detached #Parking Spaces: ______
Wheelchair Access: yes · no · ramp · elevator #Steps to Door: ______
Water: municipal · well · none Well: pump age: _____ #gal/min: ____
Waste: municipal · septic drain field/holding tank #gallons: ______
Heat: electric · gas · oil · propane · fireplace/stove · pellet stove · solar

Appointment Date/Time: __________________ Realtor's Name: __________________
Meet Location: __________________ Realtor's Number: __________________

Notes

OVERALL IMPRESSION

☆ ☆ ☆ ☆ ☆

MAKE OFFER • MAYBE • DISCARD

INDOOR EVALUATION

ROOM/LOCATION	CONDITION			NOTES
	good	fair	poor	flooring - paint - lighting
Front Entrance				
Living Room				
Dining Room				
Kitchen				
Pantry				
Family Room				
Master Bedroom				
Master Bathroom				
2nd Bedroom				
3rd Bedroom				
4th Bedroom				
Bathroom 1				
Bathroom 2				
Bathroom 3				
Laundry Area				
Mud Room				
Office/Den				
Library				
Utilities				
Basement				

EXTERIOR and YARD EVALUATION

LOCATION	NOTES
Curb Appeal	
Roof	
Windows	
Front Entrance	
Landscaping	
Trees/Shrubs	
Yard	
Lighting	
Garage	
Shed	
Deck/Patio	

OTHER CONSIDERATIONS

Neighborhood:
Cul de Sac · Dead End Road · Through Street · Rural
Safety Score: ________ Walkability Score: ________
Proximity to: Work · School · Family · Babysitter
Bus Stop · Public Transportation · Grocery Store
Schools: Elementary __________________
Middle __________________
High __________________
School District: Walk · Bus
Noise: Traffic · Business · Sirens-Police/Firehouse · Kids · Dogs
Privacy: Proximity to Neighbor · Fence · Fence Height

DECISION-MAKING WORKSHEET

Pros	Cons

Notes

HOUSE EVALUATION FORM

Address: ____________________ MLS#: __________
Neighborhood: ____________________ HOA Fees: __________ Annual Taxes: __________
Asking Price: __________ Days on the Market: ______ Square Feet: ______ Price Per Square Foot: ______
Bedrooms: __________ Lot Size: __________ Year Built: ______
Bathrooms: __________ Price Changes: ____________________

LOAN: Conv • FHA • VA • USDA • Cash • 203K
FS By Owner • REO • Foreclosure • Auction

Home Type: single family • duplex • condo • townhome • mobile
Foundation: slab • block • brick • stone • poured concrete
Basement Space: none • crawl space • partial • full • cellar
Basement: interior access • exterior access • finished • unfinished
Air Conditioning: none • central • window • mini split • fans

Garage: yes • no attached • detached #Parking Spaces: ______
Wheelchair Access: yes • no • ramp • elevator #Steps to Door: ______
Water: municipal • well • none Well: pump age: _____ #gal/min: ____
Waste: municipal • septic drain field/holding tank #gallons: ______
Heat: electric • gas • oil • propane • fireplace/stove • pellet stove • solar

Appointment Date/Time: ____________________ Realtor's Name: ____________________
Meet Location: ____________________ Realtor's Number: ____________________

Notes

OVERALL IMPRESSION

☆ ☆ ☆ ☆ ☆

MAKE OFFER • MAYBE • DISCARD

INDOOR EVALUATION

ROOM/LOCATION	CONDITION			NOTES
	good	fair	poor	flooring - paint - lighting
Front Entrance				
Living Room				
Dining Room				
Kitchen				
Pantry				
Family Room				
Master Bedroom				
Master Bathroom				
2nd Bedroom				
3rd Bedroom				
4th Bedroom				
Bathroom 1				
Bathroom 2				
Bathroom 3				
Laundry Area				
Mud Room				
Office/Den				
Library				
Utilities				
Basement				

EXTERIOR and YARD EVALUATION

LOCATION	NOTES
Curb Appeal	
Roof	
Windows	
Front Entrance	
Landscaping	
Trees/Shrubs	
Yard	
Lighting	
Garage	
Shed	
Deck/Patio	

OTHER CONSIDERATIONS

Neighborhood:
Cul de Sac • Dead End Road • Through Street • Rural
Safety Score: ________ Walkability Score: ________
Proximity to: Work • School • Family • Babysitter
Bus Stop • Public Transportation • Grocery Store
Schools: Elementary ____________________
Middle ____________________
High ____________________
School District: Walk • Bus
Noise: Traffic • Business • Sirens-Police/Firehouse • Kids • Dogs
Privacy: Proximity to Neighbor • Fence • Fence Height

DECISION-MAKING WORKSHEET

Pros	Cons

Notes

HOUSE EVALUATION FORM

Address: ____________________ MLS#: __________
Neighborhood: ____________________ HOA Fees: __________ Annual Taxes: __________
Asking Price: __________ Days on the Market: __________ Square Feet: __________ Price Per Square Foot: __________
Bedrooms: __________ Lot Size: __________ Year Built: __________
Bathrooms: __________ Price Changes: ____________________

LOAN: Conv · FHA · VA · USDA · Cash · 203K
FS By Owner · REO · Foreclosure · Auction

Home Type: single family · duplex · condo · townhome · mobile
Foundation: slab · block · brick · stone · poured concrete
Basement Space: none · crawl space · partial · full · cellar
Basement: interior access · exterior access · finished · unfinished
Air Conditioning: none · central · window · mini split · fans

Garage: yes · no attached · detached #Parking Spaces: __________
Wheelchair Access: yes · no · ramp · elevator #Steps to Door: __________
Water: municipal · well · none Well: pump age: _____ #gal/min: _____
Waste: municipal · septic drain field/holding tank #gallons: __________
Heat: electric · gas · oil · propane · fireplace/stove · pellet stove · solar

Appointment Date/Time: ____________________ Realtor's Name: ____________________
Meet Location: ____________________ Realtor's Number: ____________________

Notes

OVERALL IMPRESSION

☆ ☆ ☆ ☆ ☆

MAKE OFFER • MAYBE • DISCARD

INDOOR EVALUATION

ROOM/LOCATION	CONDITION			NOTES
	good	fair	poor	flooring - paint - lighting
Front Entrance				
Living Room				
Dining Room				
Kitchen				
Pantry				
Family Room				
Master Bedroom				
Master Bathroom				
2nd Bedroom				
3rd Bedroom				
4th Bedroom				
Bathroom 1				
Bathroom 2				
Bathroom 3				
Laundry Area				
Mud Room				
Office/Den				
Library				
Utilities				
Basement				

EXTERIOR and YARD EVALUATION

LOCATION	NOTES
Curb Appeal	
Roof	
Windows	
Front Entrance	
Landscaping	
Trees/Shrubs	
Yard	
Lighting	
Garage	
Shed	
Deck/Patio	

OTHER CONSIDERATIONS

Neighborhood:
Cul de Sac · Dead End Road · Through Street · Rural
Safety Score: __________ Walkability Score: __________
Proximity to: Work · School · Family · Babysitter
Bus Stop · Public Transportation · Grocery Store
Schools: Elementary ____________________
Middle ____________________
High ____________________
School District: Walk · Bus
Noise: Traffic · Business · Sirens-Police/Firehouse · Kids · Dogs
Privacy: Proximity to Neighbor · Fence · Fence Height

DECISION-MAKING WORKSHEET

Pros	Cons

Notes

HOUSE EVALUATION FORM

Address: ______________________ MLS#: __________
Neighborhood: ______________________ HOA Fees: __________ Annual Taxes: __________
Asking Price: __________ Days on the Market: ________ Square Feet: __________ Price Per Square Foot: __________
Bedrooms: __________ Lot Size: __________ Year Built: ________
Bathrooms: __________ Price Changes: ______________________

LOAN: Conv · FHA · VA · USDA · Cash · 203K
FS By Owner · REO · Foreclosure · Auction

Home Type: single family · duplex · condo · townhome · mobile
Foundation: slab · block · brick · stone · poured concrete
Basement Space: none · crawl space · partial · full · cellar
Basement: interior access · exterior access · finished · unfinished
Air Conditioning: none · central · window · mini split · fans

Garage: yes · no attached · detached #Parking Spaces: ________
Wheelchair Access: yes · no · ramp · elevator #Steps to Door: ________
Water: municipal · well · none Well: pump age: _____ #gal/min: ____
Waste: municipal · septic drain field/holding tank #gallons: ________
Heat: electric · gas · oil · propane · fireplace/stove · pellet stove · solar

Appointment Date/Time: ______________________ Realtor's Name: ______________________
Meet Location: ______________________ Realtor's Number: ______________________

Notes

OVERALL IMPRESSION

☆ ☆ ☆ ☆ ☆

MAKE OFFER • MAYBE • DISCARD

INDOOR EVALUATION

ROOM/LOCATION	CONDITION			NOTES
	good	fair	poor	flooring - paint - lighting
Front Entrance				
Living Room				
Dining Room				
Kitchen				
Pantry				
Family Room				
Master Bedroom				
Master Bathroom				
2nd Bedroom				
3rd Bedroom				
4th Bedroom				
Bathroom 1				
Bathroom 2				
Bathroom 3				
Laundry Area				
Mud Room				
Office/Den				
Library				
Utilities				
Basement				

EXTERIOR and YARD EVALUATION

LOCATION	NOTES
Curb Appeal	
Roof	
Windows	
Front Entrance	
Landscaping	
Trees/Shrubs	
Yard	
Lighting	
Garage	
Shed	
Deck/Patio	

OTHER CONSIDERATIONS

Neighborhood:
Cul de Sac · Dead End Road · Through Street · Rural
Safety Score: ________ Walkability Score: ________
Proximity to: Work · School · Family · Babysitter
Bus Stop · Public Transportation · Grocery Store
Schools: Elementary ______________________
Middle ______________________
High ______________________
School District: Walk · Bus
Noise: Traffic · Business · Sirens-Police/Firehouse · Kids · Dogs
Privacy: Proximity to Neighbor · Fence · Fence Height

DECISION-MAKING WORKSHEET

Pros	Cons

Notes

HOUSE EVALUATION FORM

Address: ______________________ MLS#: __________
Neighborhood: ______________________ HOA Fees: __________ Annual Taxes: __________
Asking Price: __________ Days on the Market: ______ Square Feet: __________ Price Per Square Foot: __________
Bedrooms: __________ Lot Size: __________ Year Built: ______
Bathrooms: __________ Price Changes: ______________________

LOAN: Conv • FHA • VA • USDA • Cash • 203K
FS By Owner • REO • Foreclosure • Auction

Home Type: single family • duplex • condo • townhome • mobile
Foundation: slab • block • brick • stone • poured concrete
Basement Space: none • crawl space • partial • full • cellar
Basement: interior access • exterior access • finished • unfinished
Air Conditioning: none • central • window • mini split • fans

Garage: yes • no attached • detached #Parking Spaces: ______
Wheelchair Access: yes • no • ramp • elevator #Steps to Door: ______
Water: municipal • well • none Well: pump age: _____ #gal/min: ____
Waste: municipal • septic drain field/holding tank #gallons: ______
Heat: electric • gas • oil • propane • fireplace/stove • pellet stove • solar

Appointment Date/Time: ______________________ Realtor's Name: ______________________
Meet Location: ______________________ Realtor's Number: ______________________

Notes

OVERALL IMPRESSION

☆ ☆ ☆ ☆ ☆

MAKE OFFER • MAYBE • DISCARD

INDOOR EVALUATION

ROOM/LOCATION	CONDITION			NOTES
	good	fair	poor	flooring - paint - lighting
Front Entrance				
Living Room				
Dining Room				
Kitchen				
Pantry				
Family Room				
Master Bedroom				
Master Bathroom				
2nd Bedroom				
3rd Bedroom				
4th Bedroom				
Bathroom 1				
Bathroom 2				
Bathroom 3				
Laundry Area				
Mud Room				
Office/Den				
Library				
Utilities				
Basement				

EXTERIOR and YARD EVALUATION

LOCATION	NOTES
Curb Appeal	
Roof	
Windows	
Front Entrance	
Landscaping	
Trees/Shrubs	
Yard	
Lighting	
Garage	
Shed	
Deck/Patio	

OTHER CONSIDERATIONS

Neighborhood:
Cul de Sac • Dead End Road • Through Street • Rural
Safety Score: ________ Walkability Score: ________
Proximity to: Work • School • Family • Babysitter
Bus Stop • Public Transportation • Grocery Store
Schools: Elementary ______________________
Middle ______________________
High ______________________
School District: Walk • Bus
Noise: Traffic • Business • Sirens-Police/Firehouse • Kids • Dogs
Privacy: Proximity to Neighbor • Fence • Fence Height

DECISION-MAKING WORKSHEET

Pros	Cons

Notes

HOUSE EVALUATION FORM

Address: ______________________ MLS#: ______________
Neighborhood: ______________________ HOA Fees: ____________ Annual Taxes: ______________
Asking Price: ____________ Days on the Market: ________ Square Feet: ____________ Price Per Square Foot: ____________
Bedrooms: ____________ Lot Size: ____________ Year Built: ________
Bathrooms: ____________ Price Changes: ______________________

LOAN: Conv · FHA · VA · USDA · Cash · 203K
FS By Owner · REO · Foreclosure · Auction

Home Type: single family · duplex · condo · townhome · mobile
Foundation: slab · block · brick · stone · poured concrete
Basement Space: none · crawl space · partial · full · cellar
Basement: interior access · exterior access · finished · unfinished
Air Conditioning: none · central · window · mini split · fans

Garage: yes · no attached · detached #Parking Spaces: ________
Wheelchair Access: yes · no · ramp · elevator #Steps to Door: ________
Water: municipal · well · none Well: pump age: _____ #gal/min: ____
Waste: municipal · septic drain field/holding tank #gallons: __________
Heat: electric · gas · oil · propane · fireplace/stove · pellet stove · solar

Appointment Date/Time: ______________________ Realtor's Name: ______________________
Meet Location: ______________________ Realtor's Number: ______________________

Notes

OVERALL IMPRESSION

☆☆☆☆☆

MAKE OFFER • MAYBE • DISCARD

INDOOR EVALUATION

ROOM/LOCATION	CONDITION			NOTES
	good	fair	poor	flooring - paint - lighting
Front Entrance				
Living Room				
Dining Room				
Kitchen				
Pantry				
Family Room				
Master Bedroom				
Master Bathroom				
2nd Bedroom				
3rd Bedroom				
4th Bedroom				
Bathroom 1				
Bathroom 2				
Bathroom 3				
Laundry Area				
Mud Room				
Office/Den				
Library				
Utilities				
Basement				

EXTERIOR and YARD EVALUATION

LOCATION	NOTES
Curb Appeal	
Roof	
Windows	
Front Entrance	
Landscaping	
Trees/Shrubs	
Yard	
Lighting	
Garage	
Shed	
Deck/Patio	

OTHER CONSIDERATIONS

Neighborhood:
Cul de Sac · Dead End Road · Through Street · Rural
Safety Score: ________ Walkability Score: ________
Proximity to: Work · School · Family · Babysitter
Bus Stop · Public Transportation · Grocery Store
Schools: Elementary ______________________
Middle ______________________
High ______________________
School District: Walk · Bus
Noise: Traffic · Business · Sirens-Police/Firehouse · Kids · Dogs
Privacy: Proximity to Neighbor · Fence · Fence Height

DECISION-MAKING WORKSHEET

Pros	Cons

Notes

HOUSE EVALUATION FORM

Address: ______________________________ MLS#: __________
Neighborhood: ______________________ HOA Fees: __________ Annual Taxes: __________
Asking Price: __________ Days on the Market: ________ Square Feet: __________ Price Per Square Foot: __________
Bedrooms: __________ Lot Size: __________ Year Built: ________
Bathrooms: __________ Price Changes: ______________________

LOAN: Conv • FHA • VA • USDA • Cash • 203K
FS By Owner • REO • Foreclosure • Auction

Home Type: single family • duplex • condo • townhome • mobile
Foundation: slab • block • brick • stone • poured concrete
Basement Space: none • crawl space • partial • full • cellar
Basement: interior access • exterior access • finished • unfinished
Air Conditioning: none • central • window • mini split • fans

Garage: yes • no attached • detached #Parking Spaces: ________
Wheelchair Access: yes • no • ramp • elevator #Steps to Door: ________
Water: municipal • well • none Well: pump age: _____ #gal/min: ____
Waste: municipal • septic drain field/holding tank #gallons: ________
Heat: electric • gas • oil • propane • fireplace/stove • pellet stove • solar

Appointment Date/Time: ______________________ Realtor's Name: ______________________
Meet Location: ______________________ Realtor's Number: ______________________

Notes

OVERALL IMPRESSION

☆ ☆ ☆ ☆ ☆

MAKE OFFER • MAYBE • DISCARD

INDOOR EVALUATION

ROOM/LOCATION	CONDITION			NOTES
	good	fair	poor	flooring - paint - lighting
Front Entrance				
Living Room				
Dining Room				
Kitchen				
Pantry				
Family Room				
Master Bedroom				
Master Bathroom				
2nd Bedroom				
3rd Bedroom				
4th Bedroom				
Bathroom 1				
Bathroom 2				
Bathroom 3				
Laundry Area				
Mud Room				
Office/Den				
Library				
Utilities				
Basement				

EXTERIOR and YARD EVALUATION

LOCATION	NOTES
Curb Appeal	
Roof	
Windows	
Front Entrance	
Landscaping	
Trees/Shrubs	
Yard	
Lighting	
Garage	
Shed	
Deck/Patio	

OTHER CONSIDERATIONS

Neighborhood:
Cul de Sac • Dead End Road • Through Street • Rural
Safety Score: ________ Walkability Score: ________
Proximity to: Work • School • Family • Babysitter
Bus Stop • Public Transportation • Grocery Store
Schools: Elementary ______________________
Middle ______________________
High ______________________
School District: Walk • Bus
Noise: Traffic • Business • Sirens-Police/Firehouse • Kids • Dogs
Privacy: Proximity to Neighbor • Fence • Fence Height

DECISION-MAKING WORKSHEET

Pros	Cons

Notes

HOUSE EVALUATION FORM

Address: ______________________ MLS#: __________
Neighborhood: ______________________ HOA Fees: __________ Annual Taxes: __________
Asking Price: __________ Days on the Market: __________ Square Feet: __________ Price Per Square Foot: __________
Bedrooms: __________ Lot Size: __________ Year Built: __________
Bathrooms: __________ Price Changes: ______________________

LOAN: Conv · FHA · VA · USDA · Cash · 203K
FS By Owner · REO · Foreclosure · Auction

Home Type: single family · duplex · condo · townhome · mobile
Foundation: slab · block · brick · stone · poured concrete
Basement Space: none · crawl space · partial · full · cellar
Basement: interior access · exterior access · finished · unfinished
Air Conditioning: none · central · window · mini split · fans

Garage: yes · no attached · detached #Parking Spaces: __________
Wheelchair Access: yes · no · ramp · elevator #Steps to Door: __________
Water: municipal · well · none Well: pump age: _____ #gal/min: _____
Waste: municipal · septic drain field/holding tank #gallons: __________
Heat: electric · gas · oil · propane · fireplace/stove · pellet stove · solar

Appointment Date/Time: ______________________ Realtor's Name: ______________________
Meet Location: ______________________ Realtor's Number: ______________________

Notes

OVERALL IMPRESSION

☆☆☆☆☆

MAKE OFFER • MAYBE • DISCARD

INDOOR EVALUATION

ROOM/LOCATION	CONDITION			NOTES
	good	fair	poor	flooring - paint - lighting
Front Entrance				
Living Room				
Dining Room				
Kitchen				
Pantry				
Family Room				
Master Bedroom				
Master Bathroom				
2nd Bedroom				
3rd Bedroom				
4th Bedroom				
Bathroom 1				
Bathroom 2				
Bathroom 3				
Laundry Area				
Mud Room				
Office/Den				
Library				
Utilities				
Basement				

EXTERIOR and YARD EVALUATION

LOCATION	NOTES
Curb Appeal	
Roof	
Windows	
Front Entrance	
Landscaping	
Trees/Shrubs	
Yard	
Lighting	
Garage	
Shed	
Deck/Patio	

OTHER CONSIDERATIONS

Neighborhood:
Cul de Sac · Dead End Road · Through Street · Rural
Safety Score: ________ Walkability Score: ________
Proximity to: Work · School · Family · Babysitter
Bus Stop · Public Transportation · Grocery Store
Schools: Elementary ______________________
Middle ______________________
High ______________________
School District: Walk · Bus
Noise: Traffic · Business · Sirens-Police/Firehouse · Kids · Dogs
Privacy: Proximity to Neighbor · Fence · Fence Height

DECISION-MAKING WORKSHEET

Pros	Cons

Notes

HOUSE EVALUATION FORM

Address: ______________________________ MLS#: ____________
Neighborhood: ____________________ HOA Fees: __________ Annual Taxes: __________
Asking Price: __________ Days on the Market: ______ Square Feet: __________ Price Per Square Foot: __________
Bedrooms: __________ Lot Size: __________ Year Built: ______
Bathrooms: __________ Price Changes: ____________________

LOAN: Conv · FHA · VA · USDA · Cash · 203K
FS By Owner · REO · Foreclosure · Auction

Home Type: single family · duplex · condo · townhome · mobile
Foundation: slab · block · brick · stone · poured concrete
Basement Space: none · crawl space · partial · full · cellar
Basement: interior access · exterior access · finished · unfinished
Air Conditioning: none · central · window · mini split · fans

Garage: yes · no attached · detached #Parking Spaces: ______
Wheelchair Access: yes · no · ramp · elevator #Steps to Door: ______
Water: municipal · well · none Well: pump age: _____ #gal/min: ___
Waste: municipal · septic drain field/holding tank #gallons: ______
Heat: electric · gas · oil · propane · fireplace/stove · pellet stove · solar

Appointment Date/Time: ____________________ Realtor's Name: ____________________
Meet Location: ____________________ Realtor's Number: ____________________

Notes

OVERALL IMPRESSION

☆ ☆ ☆ ☆ ☆

MAKE OFFER • MAYBE • DISCARD

INDOOR EVALUATION

ROOM/LOCATION	CONDITION			NOTES
	good	fair	poor	flooring - paint - lighting
Front Entrance				
Living Room				
Dining Room				
Kitchen				
Pantry				
Family Room				
Master Bedroom				
Master Bathroom				
2nd Bedroom				
3rd Bedroom				
4th Bedroom				
Bathroom 1				
Bathroom 2				
Bathroom 3				
Laundry Area				
Mud Room				
Office/Den				
Library				
Utilities				
Basement				

EXTERIOR and YARD EVALUATION

LOCATION	NOTES
Curb Appeal	
Roof	
Windows	
Front Entrance	
Landscaping	
Trees/Shrubs	
Yard	
Lighting	
Garage	
Shed	
Deck/Patio	

OTHER CONSIDERATIONS

Neighborhood:
Cul de Sac · Dead End Road · Through Street · Rural
Safety Score: ________ Walkability Score: ________
Proximity to: Work · School · Family · Babysitter
Bus Stop · Public Transportation · Grocery Store
Schools: Elementary ____________________
Middle ____________________
High ____________________
School District: Walk · Bus
Noise: Traffic · Business · Sirens-Police/Firehouse · Kids · Dogs
Privacy: Proximity to Neighbor · Fence · Fence Height

DECISION-MAKING WORKSHEET

Pros	Cons

Notes

HOUSE EVALUATION FORM

Address: ____________________ MLS#: __________
Neighborhood: ____________________ HOA Fees: __________ Annual Taxes: __________
Asking Price: __________ Days on the Market: ______ Square Feet: __________ Price Per Square Foot: __________
Bedrooms: __________ Lot Size: __________ Year Built: ______
Bathrooms: __________ Price Changes: ____________________

LOAN: Conv · FHA · VA · USDA · Cash · 203K
FS By Owner · REO · Foreclosure · Auction

Home Type: single family · duplex · condo · townhome · mobile
Foundation: slab · block · brick · stone · poured concrete
Basement Space: none · crawl space · partial · full · cellar
Basement: interior access · exterior access · finished · unfinished
Air Conditioning: none · central · window · mini split · fans

Garage: yes · no attached · detached #Parking Spaces: ______
Wheelchair Access: yes · no · ramp · elevator #Steps to Door: ______
Water: municipal · well · none Well: pump age: _____ #gal/min: ____
Waste: municipal · septic drain field/holding tank #gallons: ______
Heat: electric · gas · oil · propane · fireplace/stove · pellet stove · solar

Appointment Date/Time: ____________________ Realtor's Name: ____________________
Meet Location: ____________________ Realtor's Number: ____________________

Notes

OVERALL IMPRESSION

☆ ☆ ☆ ☆ ☆

MAKE OFFER • MAYBE • DISCARD

INDOOR EVALUATION

ROOM/LOCATION	CONDITION			NOTES
	good	fair	poor	flooring - paint - lighting
Front Entrance				
Living Room				
Dining Room				
Kitchen				
Pantry				
Family Room				
Master Bedroom				
Master Bathroom				
2nd Bedroom				
3rd Bedroom				
4th Bedroom				
Bathroom 1				
Bathroom 2				
Bathroom 3				
Laundry Area				
Mud Room				
Office/Den				
Library				
Utilities				
Basement				

EXTERIOR and YARD EVALUATION

LOCATION	NOTES
Curb Appeal	
Roof	
Windows	
Front Entrance	
Landscaping	
Trees/Shrubs	
Yard	
Lighting	
Garage	
Shed	
Deck/Patio	

OTHER CONSIDERATIONS

Neighborhood:
Cul de Sac · Dead End Road · Through Street · Rural
Safety Score: ______ Walkability Score: ______
Proximity to: Work · School · Family · Babysitter
Bus Stop · Public Transportation · Grocery Store
Schools: Elementary ____________________
Middle ____________________
High ____________________
School District: Walk · Bus
Noise: Traffic · Business · Sirens-Police/Firehouse · Kids · Dogs
Privacy: Proximity to Neighbor · Fence · Fence Height

DECISION-MAKING WORKSHEET

Pros	Cons

Notes

HOUSE EVALUATION FORM

Address: ______________ MLS#: ______________
Neighborhood: ______________ HOA Fees: ______________ Annual Taxes: ______________
Asking Price: ______________ Days on the Market: ______________ Square Feet: ______________ Price Per Square Foot: ______________
Bedrooms: ______________ Lot Size: ______________ Year Built: ______________
Bathrooms: ______________ Price Changes: ______________

LOAN: Conv • FHA • VA • USDA • Cash • 203K
FS By Owner • REO • Foreclosure • Auction

Home Type: single family • duplex • condo • townhome • mobile
Foundation: slab • block • brick • stone • poured concrete
Basement Space: none • crawl space • partial • full • cellar
Basement: interior access • exterior access • finished • unfinished
Air Conditioning: none • central • window • mini split • fans

Garage: yes • no attached • detached #Parking Spaces: ______
Wheelchair Access: yes • no • ramp • elevator #Steps to Door: ______
Water: municipal • well • none Well: pump age: _____ #gal/min: _____
Waste: municipal • septic drain field/holding tank #gallons: ______
Heat: electric • gas • oil • propane • fireplace/stove • pellet stove • solar

Appointment Date/Time: ______________ Realtor's Name: ______________
Meet Location: ______________ Realtor's Number: ______________

Notes

OVERALL IMPRESSION

☆ ☆ ☆ ☆ ☆

MAKE OFFER • MAYBE • DISCARD

INDOOR EVALUATION

ROOM/LOCATION	CONDITION			NOTES
	good	fair	poor	flooring - paint - lighting
Front Entrance				
Living Room				
Dining Room				
Kitchen				
Pantry				
Family Room				
Master Bedroom				
Master Bathroom				
2nd Bedroom				
3rd Bedroom				
4th Bedroom				
Bathroom 1				
Bathroom 2				
Bathroom 3				
Laundry Area				
Mud Room				
Office/Den				
Library				
Utilities				
Basement				

EXTERIOR and YARD EVALUATION

LOCATION	NOTES
Curb Appeal	
Roof	
Windows	
Front Entrance	
Landscaping	
Trees/Shrubs	
Yard	
Lighting	
Garage	
Shed	
Deck/Patio	

OTHER CONSIDERATIONS

Neighborhood:
Cul de Sac • Dead End Road • Through Street • Rural
Safety Score: ________ Walkability Score: ________
Proximity to: Work • School • Family • Babysitter
Bus Stop • Public Transportation • Grocery Store
Schools: Elementary ______________
Middle ______________
High ______________
School District: Walk • Bus
Noise: Traffic • Business • Sirens-Police/Firehouse • Kids • Dogs
Privacy: Proximity to Neighbor • Fence • Fence Height

DECISION-MAKING WORKSHEET

Pros	Cons

Notes

HOUSE EVALUATION FORM

Address: ____________ MLS#: ____________
Neighborhood: ____________ HOA Fees: ____________ Annual Taxes: ____________
Asking Price: ____________ Days on the Market: ____________ Square Feet: ____________ Price Per Square Foot: ____________
Bedrooms: ____________ Lot Size: ____________ Year Built: ____________
Bathrooms: ____________ Price Changes: ____________

LOAN: Conv · FHA · VA · USDA · Cash · 203K
FS By Owner · REO · Foreclosure · Auction

Home Type: single family · duplex · condo · townhome · mobile
Foundation: slab · block · brick · stone · poured concrete
Basement Space: none · crawl space · partial · full · cellar
Basement: interior access · exterior access · finished · unfinished
Air Conditioning: none · central · window · mini split · fans

Garage: yes · no attached · detached #Parking Spaces: ____________
Wheelchair Access: yes · no · ramp · elevator #Steps to Door: ____________
Water: municipal · well · none Well: pump age: ______ #gal/min: ______
Waste: municipal · septic drain field/holding tank #gallons: ____________
Heat: electric · gas · oil · propane · fireplace/stove · pellet stove · solar

Appointment Date/Time: ____________ Realtor's Name: ____________
Meet Location: ____________ Realtor's Number: ____________

Notes

OVERALL IMPRESSION

☆ ☆ ☆ ☆ ☆

MAKE OFFER • MAYBE • DISCARD

INDOOR EVALUATION

ROOM/LOCATION	CONDITION			NOTES
	good	fair	poor	flooring - paint - lighting
Front Entrance				
Living Room				
Dining Room				
Kitchen				
Pantry				
Family Room				
Master Bedroom				
Master Bathroom				
2nd Bedroom				
3rd Bedroom				
4th Bedroom				
Bathroom 1				
Bathroom 2				
Bathroom 3				
Laundry Area				
Mud Room				
Office/Den				
Library				
Utilities				
Basement				

EXTERIOR and YARD EVALUATION

LOCATION	NOTES
Curb Appeal	
Roof	
Windows	
Front Entrance	
Landscaping	
Trees/Shrubs	
Yard	
Lighting	
Garage	
Shed	
Deck/Patio	

OTHER CONSIDERATIONS

Neighborhood:
Cul de Sac · Dead End Road · Through Street · Rural
Safety Score: ____________ Walkability Score: ____________
Proximity to: Work · School · Family · Babysitter
Bus Stop · Public Transportation · Grocery Store
Schools: Elementary ____________
Middle ____________
High ____________
School District: Walk · Bus
Noise: Traffic · Business · Sirens-Police/Firehouse · Kids · Dogs
Privacy: Proximity to Neighbor · Fence · Fence Height

DECISION-MAKING WORKSHEET

Pros	Cons

Notes

HOUSE EVALUATION FORM

Address: ______________________ MLS#: __________
Neighborhood: ______________________ HOA Fees: __________ Annual Taxes: __________
Asking Price: __________ Days on the Market: ______ Square Feet: __________ Price Per Square Foot: __________
Bedrooms: __________ Lot Size: __________ Year Built: ______
Bathrooms: __________ Price Changes: ______________

LOAN: Conv · FHA · VA · USDA · Cash · 203K
FS By Owner · REO · Foreclosure · Auction

Home Type: single family · duplex · condo · townhome · mobile
Foundation: slab · block · brick · stone · poured concrete
Basement Space: none · crawl space · partial · full · cellar
Basement: interior access · exterior access · finished · unfinished
Air Conditioning: none · central · window · mini split · fans

Garage: yes · no attached · detached #Parking Spaces: ______
Wheelchair Access: yes · no · ramp · elevator #Steps to Door: ______
Water: municipal · well · none Well: pump age: ____ #gal/min: ___
Waste: municipal · septic drain field/holding tank #gallons: ______
Heat: electric · gas · oil · propane · fireplace/stove · pellet stove · solar

Appointment Date/Time: ______________ Realtor's Name: ______________
Meet Location: ______________ Realtor's Number: ______________

Notes

OVERALL IMPRESSION

☆ ☆ ☆ ☆ ☆

MAKE OFFER • MAYBE • DISCARD

INDOOR EVALUATION

ROOM/LOCATION	CONDITION			NOTES
	good	fair	poor	flooring - paint - lighting
Front Entrance				
Living Room				
Dining Room				
Kitchen				
Pantry				
Family Room				
Master Bedroom				
Master Bathroom				
2nd Bedroom				
3rd Bedroom				
4th Bedroom				
Bathroom 1				
Bathroom 2				
Bathroom 3				
Laundry Area				
Mud Room				
Office/Den				
Library				
Utilities				
Basement				

EXTERIOR and YARD EVALUATION

LOCATION	NOTES
Curb Appeal	
Roof	
Windows	
Front Entrance	
Landscaping	
Trees/Shrubs	
Yard	
Lighting	
Garage	
Shed	
Deck/Patio	

OTHER CONSIDERATIONS

Neighborhood:
Cul de Sac · Dead End Road · Through Street · Rural
Safety Score: ______ Walkability Score: ______
Proximity to: Work · School · Family · Babysitter
Bus Stop · Public Transportation · Grocery Store
Schools: Elementary ______________
Middle ______________
High ______________
School District: Walk · Bus
Noise: Traffic · Business · Sirens-Police/Firehouse · Kids · Dogs
Privacy: Proximity to Neighbor · Fence · Fence Height

DECISION-MAKING WORKSHEET

Pros	Cons

Notes

HOUSE EVALUATION FORM

Address: ______________________ MLS#: __________
Neighborhood: ______________________ HOA Fees: __________ Annual Taxes: __________
Asking Price: __________ Days on the Market: __________ Square Feet: __________ Price Per Square Foot: __________
Bedrooms: __________ Lot Size: __________ Year Built: __________
Bathrooms: __________ Price Changes: ______________________

LOAN: Conv · FHA · VA · USDA · Cash · 203K
FS By Owner · REO · Foreclosure · Auction

Home Type: single family · duplex · condo · townhome · mobile
Foundation: slab · block · brick · stone · poured concrete
Basement Space: none · crawl space · partial · full · cellar
Basement: interior access · exterior access · finished · unfinished
Air Conditioning: none · central · window · mini split · fans

Garage: yes · no attached · detached #Parking Spaces: ______
Wheelchair Access: yes · no · ramp · elevator #Steps to Door: ______
Water: municipal · well · none Well: pump age: _____ #gal/min: ____
Waste: municipal · septic drain field/holding tank #gallons: ________
Heat: electric · gas · oil · propane · fireplace/stove · pellet stove · solar

Appointment Date/Time: ______________________ Realtor's Name: ______________________
Meet Location: ______________________ Realtor's Number: ______________________

Notes

OVERALL IMPRESSION

☆ ☆ ☆ ☆ ☆

MAKE OFFER • MAYBE • DISCARD

INDOOR EVALUATION

ROOM/LOCATION	CONDITION			NOTES
	good	fair	poor	flooring - paint - lighting
Front Entrance				
Living Room				
Dining Room				
Kitchen				
Pantry				
Family Room				
Master Bedroom				
Master Bathroom				
2nd Bedroom				
3rd Bedroom				
4th Bedroom				
Bathroom 1				
Bathroom 2				
Bathroom 3				
Laundry Area				
Mud Room				
Office/Den				
Library				
Utilities				
Basement				

EXTERIOR and YARD EVALUATION

LOCATION	NOTES
Curb Appeal	
Roof	
Windows	
Front Entrance	
Landscaping	
Trees/Shrubs	
Yard	
Lighting	
Garage	
Shed	
Deck/Patio	

OTHER CONSIDERATIONS

Neighborhood:
Cul de Sac · Dead End Road · Through Street · Rural
Safety Score: ________ Walkability Score: ________
Proximity to: Work · School · Family · Babysitter
Bus Stop · Public Transportation · Grocery Store
Schools: Elementary ______________________
Middle ______________________
High ______________________
School District: Walk · Bus
Noise: Traffic · Business · Sirens-Police/Firehouse · Kids · Dogs
Privacy: Proximity to Neighbor · Fence · Fence Height

DECISION-MAKING WORKSHEET

Pros	Cons

Notes

HOUSE EVALUATION FORM

Address: ______________________ MLS#: __________
Neighborhood: ______________________ HOA Fees: __________ Annual Taxes: __________
Asking Price: __________ Days on the Market: __________ Square Feet: __________ Price Per Square Foot: __________
Bedrooms: __________ Lot Size: __________ Year Built: __________
Bathrooms: __________ Price Changes: __________

LOAN: Conv · FHA · VA · USDA · Cash · 203K
FS By Owner · REO · Foreclosure · Auction

Home Type: single family · duplex · condo · townhome · mobile
Foundation: slab · block · brick · stone · poured concrete
Basement Space: none · crawl space · partial · full · cellar
Basement: interior access · exterior access · finished · unfinished
Air Conditioning: none · central · window · mini split · fans

Garage: yes · no attached · detached #Parking Spaces: __________
Wheelchair Access: yes · no · ramp · elevator #Steps to Door: __________
Water: municipal · well · none Well: pump age: _____ #gal/min: _____
Waste: municipal · septic drain field/holding tank #gallons: __________
Heat: electric · gas · oil · propane · fireplace/stove · pellet stove · solar

Appointment Date/Time: __________ Realtor's Name: __________
Meet Location: __________ Realtor's Number: __________

Notes

OVERALL IMPRESSION

☆ ☆ ☆ ☆ ☆

MAKE OFFER • MAYBE • DISCARD

INDOOR EVALUATION

ROOM/LOCATION	CONDITION			NOTES
	good	fair	poor	flooring - paint - lighting
Front Entrance				
Living Room				
Dining Room				
Kitchen				
Pantry				
Family Room				
Master Bedroom				
Master Bathroom				
2nd Bedroom				
3rd Bedroom				
4th Bedroom				
Bathroom 1				
Bathroom 2				
Bathroom 3				
Laundry Area				
Mud Room				
Office/Den				
Library				
Utilities				
Basement				

EXTERIOR and YARD EVALUATION

LOCATION	NOTES
Curb Appeal	
Roof	
Windows	
Front Entrance	
Landscaping	
Trees/Shrubs	
Yard	
Lighting	
Garage	
Shed	
Deck/Patio	

OTHER CONSIDERATIONS

Neighborhood:
Cul de Sac · Dead End Road · Through Street · Rural
Safety Score: __________ Walkability Score: __________
Proximity to: Work · School · Family · Babysitter
Bus Stop · Public Transportation · Grocery Store
Schools: Elementary __________
Middle __________
High __________
School District: Walk · Bus
Noise: Traffic · Business · Sirens-Police/Firehouse · Kids · Dogs
Privacy: Proximity to Neighbor · Fence · Fence Height

DECISION-MAKING WORKSHEET

Pros	Cons

Notes

HOUSE EVALUATION FORM

Address: ______________________ MLS#: __________
Neighborhood: ______________________ HOA Fees: __________ Annual Taxes: __________
Asking Price: __________ Days on the Market: ______ Square Feet: __________ Price Per Square Foot: __________
Bedrooms: __________ Lot Size: __________ Year Built: ______
Bathrooms: __________ Price Changes: ______________

LOAN: Conv · FHA · VA · USDA · Cash · 203K
FS By Owner · REO · Foreclosure · Auction

Home Type: single family · duplex · condo · townhome · mobile
Foundation: slab · block · brick · stone · poured concrete
Basement Space: none · crawl space · partial · full · cellar
Basement: interior access · exterior access · finished · unfinished
Air Conditioning: none · central · window · mini split · fans

Garage: yes · no attached · detached #Parking Spaces: ______
Wheelchair Access: yes · no · ramp · elevator #Steps to Door: ______
Water: municipal · well · none Well: pump age: _____ #gal/min: ____
Waste: municipal · septic drain field/holding tank #gallons: ________
Heat: electric · gas · oil · propane · fireplace/stove · pellet stove · solar

Appointment Date/Time: ______________ Realtor's Name: ______________
Meet Location: ______________ Realtor's Number: ______________

Notes

OVERALL IMPRESSION

☆ ☆ ☆ ☆ ☆

MAKE OFFER • MAYBE • DISCARD

INDOOR EVALUATION

ROOM/LOCATION	CONDITION			NOTES
	good	fair	poor	flooring - paint - lighting
Front Entrance				
Living Room				
Dining Room				
Kitchen				
Pantry				
Family Room				
Master Bedroom				
Master Bathroom				
2nd Bedroom				
3rd Bedroom				
4th Bedroom				
Bathroom 1				
Bathroom 2				
Bathroom 3				
Laundry Area				
Mud Room				
Office/Den				
Library				
Utilities				
Basement				

EXTERIOR and YARD EVALUATION

LOCATION	NOTES
Curb Appeal	
Roof	
Windows	
Front Entrance	
Landscaping	
Trees/Shrubs	
Yard	
Lighting	
Garage	
Shed	
Deck/Patio	

OTHER CONSIDERATIONS

Neighborhood:
Cul de Sac · Dead End Road · Through Street · Rural
Safety Score: ________ Walkability Score: ________
Proximity to: Work · School · Family · Babysitter
Bus Stop · Public Transportation · Grocery Store
Schools: Elementary ______________
Middle ______________
High ______________
School District: Walk · Bus
Noise: Traffic · Business · Sirens-Police/Firehouse · Kids · Dogs
Privacy: Proximity to Neighbor · Fence · Fence Height

DECISION-MAKING WORKSHEET

Pros	Cons

Notes

HOUSE EVALUATION FORM

Address: ______________________________ MLS#: __________
Neighborhood: ______________________ HOA Fees: __________ Annual Taxes: __________
Asking Price: __________ Days on the Market: ______ Square Feet: __________ Price Per Square Foot: __________
Bedrooms: __________ Lot Size: __________ Year Built: ______
Bathrooms: __________ Price Changes: ______________________

LOAN: Conv · FHA · VA · USDA · Cash · 203K
FS By Owner · REO · Foreclosure · Auction

Home Type: single family · duplex · condo · townhome · mobile
Foundation: slab · block · brick · stone · poured concrete
Basement Space: none · crawl space · partial · full · cellar
Basement: interior access · exterior access · finished · unfinished
Air Conditioning: none · central · window · mini split · fans

Garage: yes · no attached · detached #Parking Spaces: ______
Wheelchair Access: yes · no · ramp · elevator #Steps to Door: ______
Water: municipal · well · none Well: pump age: _____ #gal/min: ____
Waste: municipal · septic drain field/holding tank #gallons: ________
Heat: electric · gas · oil · propane · fireplace/stove · pellet stove · solar

Appointment Date/Time: ______________________ Realtor's Name: ______________________
Meet Location: ______________________ Realtor's Number: ______________________

Notes

OVERALL IMPRESSION

☆☆☆☆☆

MAKE OFFER • MAYBE • DISCARD

INDOOR EVALUATION

ROOM/LOCATION	CONDITION			NOTES
	good	fair	poor	flooring - paint - lighting
Front Entrance				
Living Room				
Dining Room				
Kitchen				
Pantry				
Family Room				
Master Bedroom				
Master Bathroom				
2nd Bedroom				
3rd Bedroom				
4th Bedroom				
Bathroom 1				
Bathroom 2				
Bathroom 3				
Laundry Area				
Mud Room				
Office/Den				
Library				
Utilities				
Basement				

EXTERIOR and YARD EVALUATION

LOCATION	NOTES
Curb Appeal	
Roof	
Windows	
Front Entrance	
Landscaping	
Trees/Shrubs	
Yard	
Lighting	
Garage	
Shed	
Deck/Patio	

OTHER CONSIDERATIONS

Neighborhood:
Cul de Sac · Dead End Road · Through Street · Rural
Safety Score: ________ Walkability Score: ________
Proximity to: Work · School · Family · Babysitter
Bus Stop · Public Transportation · Grocery Store
Schools: Elementary ______________________
Middle ______________________
High ______________________
School District: Walk · Bus
Noise: Traffic · Business · Sirens-Police/Firehouse · Kids · Dogs
Privacy: Proximity to Neighbor · Fence · Fence Height

DECISION-MAKING WORKSHEET

Pros	Cons

Notes

HOUSE EVALUATION FORM

Address: ______________________ MLS#: __________
Neighborhood: ______________________ HOA Fees: __________ Annual Taxes: __________
Asking Price: __________ Days on the Market: ________ Square Feet: __________ Price Per Square Foot: __________
Bedrooms: __________ Lot Size: __________ Year Built: ________
Bathrooms: __________ Price Changes: ______________________

LOAN: Conv · FHA · VA · USDA · Cash · 203K
FS By Owner · REO · Foreclosure · Auction

Home Type: single family · duplex · condo · townhome · mobile
Foundation: slab · block · brick · stone · poured concrete
Basement Space: none · crawl space · partial · full · cellar
Basement: interior access · exterior access · finished · unfinished
Air Conditioning: none · central · window · mini split · fans

Garage: yes · no attached · detached #Parking Spaces: ________
Wheelchair Access: yes · no · ramp · elevator #Steps to Door: ________
Water: municipal · well · none Well: pump age: _____ #gal/min: ____
Waste: municipal · septic drain field/holding tank #gallons: __________
Heat: electric · gas · oil · propane · fireplace/stove · pellet stove · solar

Appointment Date/Time: ______________________ Realtor's Name: ______________________
Meet Location: ______________________ Realtor's Number: ______________________

Notes

OVERALL IMPRESSION

☆ ☆ ☆ ☆ ☆

MAKE OFFER • MAYBE • DISCARD

INDOOR EVALUATION

ROOM/LOCATION	CONDITION			NOTES
	good	fair	poor	flooring - paint - lighting
Front Entrance				
Living Room				
Dining Room				
Kitchen				
Pantry				
Family Room				
Master Bedroom				
Master Bathroom				
2nd Bedroom				
3rd Bedroom				
4th Bedroom				
Bathroom 1				
Bathroom 2				
Bathroom 3				
Laundry Area				
Mud Room				
Office/Den				
Library				
Utilities				
Basement				

EXTERIOR and YARD EVALUATION

LOCATION	NOTES
Curb Appeal	
Roof	
Windows	
Front Entrance	
Landscaping	
Trees/Shrubs	
Yard	
Lighting	
Garage	
Shed	
Deck/Patio	

OTHER CONSIDERATIONS

Neighborhood:
Cul de Sac · Dead End Road · Through Street · Rural
Safety Score: ________ Walkability Score: ________
Proximity to: Work · School · Family · Babysitter
Bus Stop · Public Transportation · Grocery Store
Schools: Elementary ______________________
Middle ______________________
High ______________________
School District: Walk · Bus
Noise: Traffic · Business · Sirens-Police/Firehouse · Kids · Dogs
Privacy: Proximity to Neighbor · Fence · Fence Height

DECISION-MAKING WORKSHEET

Pros	Cons

Notes

HOUSE EVALUATION FORM

Address: ____________________ MLS#: ____________
Neighborhood: ____________________ HOA Fees: ____________ Annual Taxes: ____________
Asking Price: ____________ Days on the Market: ________ Square Feet: ____________ Price Per Square Foot: ____________
Bedrooms: ____________ Lot Size: ____________ Year Built: ________
Bathrooms: ____________ Price Changes: ____________________

LOAN: Conv · FHA · VA · USDA · Cash · 203K
FS By Owner · REO · Foreclosure · Auction

Home Type: single family · duplex · condo · townhome · mobile
Foundation: slab · block · brick · stone · poured concrete
Basement Space: none · crawl space · partial · full · cellar
Basement: interior access · exterior access · finished · unfinished
Air Conditioning: none · central · window · mini split · fans

Garage: yes · no attached · detached #Parking Spaces: ________
Wheelchair Access: yes · no · ramp · elevator #Steps to Door: ________
Water: municipal · well · none Well: pump age: _____ #gal/min: ____
Waste: municipal · septic drain field/holding tank #gallons: ________
Heat: electric · gas · oil · propane · fireplace/stove · pellet stove · solar

Appointment Date/Time: ____________________ Realtor's Name: ____________________
Meet Location: ____________________ Realtor's Number: ____________________

Notes

OVERALL IMPRESSION

☆ ☆ ☆ ☆ ☆

MAKE OFFER • MAYBE • DISCARD

INDOOR EVALUATION

ROOM/LOCATION	CONDITION			NOTES
	good	fair	poor	flooring - paint - lighting
Front Entrance				
Living Room				
Dining Room				
Kitchen				
Pantry				
Family Room				
Master Bedroom				
Master Bathroom				
2nd Bedroom				
3rd Bedroom				
4th Bedroom				
Bathroom 1				
Bathroom 2				
Bathroom 3				
Laundry Area				
Mud Room				
Office/Den				
Library				
Utilities				
Basement				

EXTERIOR and YARD EVALUATION

LOCATION	NOTES
Curb Appeal	
Roof	
Windows	
Front Entrance	
Landscaping	
Trees/Shrubs	
Yard	
Lighting	
Garage	
Shed	
Deck/Patio	

OTHER CONSIDERATIONS

Neighborhood:
Cul de Sac · Dead End Road · Through Street · Rural
Safety Score: ________ Walkability Score: ________
Proximity to: Work · School · Family · Babysitter
Bus Stop · Public Transportation · Grocery Store
Schools: Elementary ____________________
Middle ____________________
High ____________________
School District: Walk · Bus
Noise: Traffic · Business · Sirens-Police/Firehouse · Kids · Dogs
Privacy: Proximity to Neighbor · Fence · Fence Height

DECISION-MAKING WORKSHEET

Pros	Cons

Notes

HOUSE EVALUATION FORM

Address: ______ MLS#: ______
Neighborhood: ______ HOA Fees: ______ Annual Taxes: ______
Asking Price: ______ Days on the Market: ______ Square Feet: ______ Price Per Square Foot: ______
Bedrooms: ______ Lot Size: ______ Year Built: ______
Bathrooms: ______ Price Changes: ______

LOAN: Conv · FHA · VA · USDA · Cash · 203K
FS By Owner · REO · Foreclosure · Auction

Home Type: single family · duplex · condo · townhome · mobile
Foundation: slab · block · brick · stone · poured concrete
Basement Space: none · crawl space · partial · full · cellar
Basement: interior access · exterior access · finished · unfinished
Air Conditioning: none · central · window · mini split · fans

Garage: yes · no attached · detached #Parking Spaces: ______
Wheelchair Access: yes · no · ramp · elevator #Steps to Door: ______
Water: municipal · well · none Well: pump age: ______ #gal/min: ______
Waste: municipal · septic drain field/holding tank #gallons: ______
Heat: electric · gas · oil · propane · fireplace/stove · pellet stove · solar

Appointment Date/Time: ______ Realtor's Name: ______
Meet Location: ______ Realtor's Number: ______

Notes

OVERALL IMPRESSION

☆ ☆ ☆ ☆ ☆

MAKE OFFER • MAYBE • DISCARD

INDOOR EVALUATION

ROOM/LOCATION	CONDITION			NOTES
	good	fair	poor	flooring - paint - lighting
Front Entrance				
Living Room				
Dining Room				
Kitchen				
Pantry				
Family Room				
Master Bedroom				
Master Bathroom				
2nd Bedroom				
3rd Bedroom				
4th Bedroom				
Bathroom 1				
Bathroom 2				
Bathroom 3				
Laundry Area				
Mud Room				
Office/Den				
Library				
Utilities				
Basement				

EXTERIOR and YARD EVALUATION

LOCATION	NOTES
Curb Appeal	
Roof	
Windows	
Front Entrance	
Landscaping	
Trees/Shrubs	
Yard	
Lighting	
Garage	
Shed	
Deck/Patio	

OTHER CONSIDERATIONS

Neighborhood:
Cul de Sac · Dead End Road · Through Street · Rural
Safety Score: ______ Walkability Score: ______
Proximity to: Work · School · Family · Babysitter
Bus Stop · Public Transportation · Grocery Store
Schools: Elementary ______
Middle ______
High ______
School District: Walk · Bus
Noise: Traffic · Business · Sirens-Police/Firehouse · Kids · Dogs
Privacy: Proximity to Neighbor · Fence · Fence Height

DECISION-MAKING WORKSHEET

Pros	Cons

Notes

HOUSE EVALUATION FORM

Address: ______________________________ MLS#: ____________
Neighborhood: ______________________ HOA Fees: __________ Annual Taxes: __________
Asking Price: __________ Days on the Market: ________ Square Feet: __________ Price Per Square Foot: __________
Bedrooms: __________ Lot Size: __________ Year Built: ________
Bathrooms: __________ Price Changes: ______________________

LOAN: Conv · FHA · VA · USDA · Cash · 203K
FS By Owner · REO · Foreclosure · Auction

Home Type: single family · duplex · condo · townhome · mobile
Foundation: slab · block · brick · stone · poured concrete
Basement Space: none · crawl space · partial · full · cellar
Basement: interior access · exterior access · finished · unfinished
Air Conditioning: none · central · window · mini split · fans

Garage: yes · no attached · detached #Parking Spaces: ________
Wheelchair Access: yes · no · ramp · elevator #Steps to Door: ________
Water: municipal · well · none Well: pump age: _____ #gal/min: ____
Waste: municipal · septic drain field/holding tank #gallons: __________
Heat: electric · gas · oil · propane · fireplace/stove · pellet stove · solar

Appointment Date/Time: ______________________ Realtor's Name: ______________________
Meet Location: ______________________ Realtor's Number: ______________________

Notes

OVERALL IMPRESSION

☆ ☆ ☆ ☆ ☆

MAKE OFFER • MAYBE • DISCARD

INDOOR EVALUATION

ROOM/LOCATION	CONDITION			NOTES
	good	fair	poor	flooring - paint - lighting
Front Entrance				
Living Room				
Dining Room				
Kitchen				
Pantry				
Family Room				
Master Bedroom				
Master Bathroom				
2nd Bedroom				
3rd Bedroom				
4th Bedroom				
Bathroom 1				
Bathroom 2				
Bathroom 3				
Laundry Area				
Mud Room				
Office/Den				
Library				
Utilities				
Basement				

EXTERIOR and YARD EVALUATION

LOCATION	NOTES
Curb Appeal	
Roof	
Windows	
Front Entrance	
Landscaping	
Trees/Shrubs	
Yard	
Lighting	
Garage	
Shed	
Deck/Patio	

OTHER CONSIDERATIONS

Neighborhood:
Cul de Sac · Dead End Road · Through Street · Rural
Safety Score: ________ Walkability Score: ________
Proximity to: Work · School · Family · Babysitter
Bus Stop · Public Transportation · Grocery Store
Schools: Elementary ______________________
Middle ______________________
High ______________________
School District: Walk · Bus
Noise: Traffic · Business · Sirens-Police/Firehouse · Kids · Dogs
Privacy: Proximity to Neighbor · Fence · Fence Height

DECISION-MAKING WORKSHEET

Pros	Cons

Notes

HOUSE EVALUATION FORM

Address: ______ MLS#: ______
Neighborhood: ______ HOA Fees: ______ Annual Taxes: ______
Asking Price: ______ Days on the Market: ______ Square Feet: ______ Price Per Square Foot: ______
Bedrooms: ______ Lot Size: ______ Year Built: ______
Bathrooms: ______ Price Changes: ______

LOAN: Conv · FHA · VA · USDA · Cash · 203K
FS By Owner · REO · Foreclosure · Auction

Home Type: single family · duplex · condo · townhome · mobile
Foundation: slab · block · brick · stone · poured concrete
Basement Space: none · crawl space · partial · full · cellar
Basement: interior access · exterior access · finished · unfinished
Air Conditioning: none · central · window · mini split · fans

Garage: yes · no attached · detached #Parking Spaces: ______
Wheelchair Access: yes · no · ramp · elevator #Steps to Door: ______
Water: municipal · well · none Well: pump age: ______ #gal/min: ______
Waste: municipal · septic drain field/holding tank #gallons: ______
Heat: electric · gas · oil · propane · fireplace/stove · pellet stove · solar

Appointment Date/Time: ______ Realtor's Name: ______
Meet Location: ______ Realtor's Number: ______

Notes

OVERALL IMPRESSION

☆ ☆ ☆ ☆ ☆

MAKE OFFER • MAYBE • DISCARD

INDOOR EVALUATION

ROOM/LOCATION	CONDITION			NOTES
	good	fair	poor	flooring - paint - lighting
Front Entrance				
Living Room				
Dining Room				
Kitchen				
Pantry				
Family Room				
Master Bedroom				
Master Bathroom				
2nd Bedroom				
3rd Bedroom				
4th Bedroom				
Bathroom 1				
Bathroom 2				
Bathroom 3				
Laundry Area				
Mud Room				
Office/Den				
Library				
Utilities				
Basement				

EXTERIOR and YARD EVALUATION

LOCATION	NOTES
Curb Appeal	
Roof	
Windows	
Front Entrance	
Landscaping	
Trees/Shrubs	
Yard	
Lighting	
Garage	
Shed	
Deck/Patio	

OTHER CONSIDERATIONS

Neighborhood:
Cul de Sac · Dead End Road · Through Street · Rural
Safety Score: ______ Walkability Score: ______
Proximity to: Work · School · Family · Babysitter
Bus Stop · Public Transportation · Grocery Store
Schools: Elementary ______
Middle ______
High ______
School District: Walk · Bus
Noise: Traffic · Business · Sirens-Police/Firehouse · Kids · Dogs
Privacy: Proximity to Neighbor · Fence · Fence Height

NEW HOME MORTGAGE & LOAN WORKSHEET

FICO SCORE

Financial Institution: Loan Officer Name & Ph #:		
Amount Borrowed:		
Mortgage Rate:		
Loan Type:	Conv • FHA • VA • USDA • 203K	Conv • FHA • VA • USDA • 203K
Loan Term:	5 yr • 15 yr • 20 yr • 30 yr	5 yr • 15 yr • 20 yr • 30 yr
	Fixed Rate Adjustable Rate	Fixed Rate Adjustable Rate
Downpayment Amount		
ESCROW	Mortgage Insurance (PMI): $	Mortgage Insurance (PMI): $
	Taxes: $	Taxes: $
	Home Insurance: $	Home Insurance: $
Monthly Payment:		
Total Borrowed:		
Amount Paid at Completion:		
Early Pay-off Penalty?	Yes No	Yes No
Addt'l Payments Allowed?	Yes No	Yes No
Payments Allowed:	Monthly - Weekly - Bi-Monthly	Monthly - Weekly - Bi-Monthly

Financial Institution: Loan Officer Name & Ph #:		
Amount Borrowed:		
Mortgage Rate:		
Loan Type:	Conv • FHA • VA • USDA • 203K	Conv • FHA • VA • USDA • 203K
Loan Term:	5 yr • 15 yr • 20 yr • 30 yr	5 yr • 15 yr • 20 yr • 30 yr
	Fixed Rate Adjustable Rate	Fixed Rate Adjustable Rate
Downpayment Amount		
ESCROW	Mortgage Insurance (PMI): $	Mortgage Insurance (PMI): $
	Taxes: $	Taxes: $
	Home Insurance: $	Home Insurance: $
Monthly Payment:		
Total Borrowed:		
Amount Paid at Completion:		
Early Pay-off Penalty?	Yes No	Yes No
Addt'l Payments Allowed?	Yes No	Yes No
Payments Allowed:	Monthly - Weekly - Bi-Monthly	Monthly - Weekly - Bi-Monthly

NEW HOME MORTGAGE & LOAN WORKSHEET

FICO SCORE [ ]

Financial Institution: Loan Officer Name & Ph #:		
Amount Borrowed:		
Mortgage Rate:		
Loan Type:	Conv • FHA • VA • USDA • 203K	Conv • FHA • VA • USDA • 203K
Loan Term:	5 yr • 15 yr • 20 yr • 30 yr	5 yr • 15 yr • 20 yr • 30 yr
	Fixed Rate Adjustable Rate	Fixed Rate Adjustable Rate
Downpayment Amount		
ESCROW	Mortgage Insurance (PMI): $	Mortgage Insurance (PMI): $
	Taxes: $	Taxes: $
	Home Insurance: $	Home Insurance: $
Monthly Payment:		
Total Borrowed:		
Amount Paid at Completion:		
Early Pay-off Penalty?	Yes No	Yes No
Addt'l Payments Allowed?	Yes No	Yes No
Payments Allowed:	Monthly - Weekly - Bi-Monthly	Monthly - Weekly - Bi-Monthly

Financial Institution: Loan Officer Name & Ph #:		
Amount Borrowed:		
Mortgage Rate:		
Loan Type:	Conv • FHA • VA • USDA • 203K	Conv • FHA • VA • USDA • 203K
Loan Term:	5 yr • 15 yr • 20 yr • 30 yr	5 yr • 15 yr • 20 yr • 30 yr
	Fixed Rate Adjustable Rate	Fixed Rate Adjustable Rate
Downpayment Amount		
ESCROW	Mortgage Insurance (PMI): $	Mortgage Insurance (PMI): $
	Taxes: $	Taxes: $
	Home Insurance: $	Home Insurance: $
Monthly Payment:		
Total Borrowed:		
Amount Paid at Completion:		
Early Pay-off Penalty?	Yes No	Yes No
Addt'l Payments Allowed?	Yes No	Yes No
Payments Allowed:	Monthly - Weekly - Bi-Monthly	Monthly - Weekly - Bi-Monthly

RELOCATION PLANNING

Old Address:

Old Phone Number:

Move-in Date:
Move-out Date:
Mortgage/Rent Amount:
Landlord:
Mortgage Company:

Notes:

New Address:

New Phone Number:

Settlement Date:
Move-in Date:
Mortgage/Rent Amount:
Landlord:
Mortgage Company:

Notes:

Appraiser Name:
Appraiser Ph #:

Home Inspector Name:
Home Inspector Ph #:

Survey/Land Deed:

Tax Information:

Title Company:
Title Company Address:

Title Contact Name & Ph#:

Settlement Date & Time:
Amount Due at Settlement:
Settlement Location:

Mortgage Company:
Loan Officer Name & Ph #:
Loan Type: Conventional • FHA • VA • USDA • 203K   Loan Term: 5 yr • 15 yr • 20 yr • 30 yr   Mortgage Rate:

Borrower #1:
Borrower #2:
Borrower #3:
Borrower #4:

Total Borrowed: $________________ Monthly Payment: $ ______________ First Payment Due Date:
(Mortgage Insurance (PMI): $__________ Taxes: $__________ Home Insurance: $ __________)

Home Insurance Provider:
Insurance Agent:
Insurance Contact #:
Rider &/or Additional Insurance:

Home Insurance Annual Cost:
Policy #:
Insured Amount:

Wildrose Media website
Home Page

Faith Family Fun Blog

Wildrose Media website
Shop Page

Additional books from Wildrose Media, available on Amazon:

Sermon Notebook
Kids Ages 9-12 years
Cross cover

Sermon Notebook
Kids Ages 6-8 years
Bunny cover

The Birth of Jesus
Coloring Book

The Story of Easter
Coloring Book
Blue cover

Bible Teaching
Sheets
Old Testament - KJV

Bible Teaching Sheets
New Testament - KJV

Friendship and Freedom
Story of the Statue of Liberty

100 Questions to Ask Myself
Vol.1 - pink cover

Ultimate Fishing Journal
for Kids Vol. 1

Ultimate Fishing Journal
for Girls - pink cover

Headache Diary, 5"x 6"
Symptom Notebook

Dutch Boy & Girl
Small Notebook 5"x6"

Made in the USA
Monee, IL
04 November 2026

67380152R00039